The Council of Chief State School Officers is a nonpartisan, nationwide, nonprofit organization of public officials who head departments of elementary and secondary education in the states, the District of Columbia, the Department of Defense Education Activity, and five U.S. extra-state jurisdictions. CCSSO provides leadership, advocacy, and technical assistance on major educational issues. The Council seeks member consensus on major educational issues and expresses their views to civic and professional organizations, federal agencies, Congress, and the public.

For information about how to obtain copies of this document please visit http://www.ccsso.org/intasc.

Council of Chief State School Officers
One Massachusetts Avenue, NW, Suite 700
Washington, DC 20001-1431
Phone: 202-336-7000
Fax: 202-408-1938

Suggested Citation:

Council of Chief State School Officers. (2011, April). Interstate Teacher Assessment and Support Consortium (InTASC) Model Core Teaching Standards: A Resource for State Dialogue. Washington, DC: Author.

Copyright © 2011 by the Council of Chief State School Officers, Washington, DC.

Table of Contents

Acknowledgements 2

Introduction 3

Summary of Standards 8

The Learner and Learning

    Standard #1: Learner Development 10

    Standard #2: Learning Differences 11

    Standard #3: Learning Environments 12

Content Knowledge

    Standard #4: Content Knowledge 13

    Standard #5: Application of Content 14

Instructional Practice

    Standard #6: Assessment 15

    Standard #7: Planning for Instruction 16

    Standard #8: Instructional Strategies 17

Professional Responsibility

    Standard #9: Professional Learning and Ethical Practice 18

    Standard #10: Leadership and Collaboration 19

Glossary of Terms 20

Reference Chart of Key Cross-Cutting Themes 23

InTASC Model Core Standards Update Committee 24

Acknowledgements

InTASC would like to express its sincere appreciation to the National Education Association, the Educational Testing Service, and Evaluation Systems group of Pearson for providing the funding for this project.

We would also like to offer a special thanks to all the InTASC Core Standards Update Committee members who enthusiastically volunteered their time and energy to the challenging task of describing what effective teaching across all content areas and grade levels looks like today. InTASC depends upon the support and input from practicing teachers, teacher educators, and other education professionals such as those on our committee to effectively pursue our mission of providing resources to guide state education policy.

Finally, InTASC would like to acknowledge and thank the many national education organizations who worked with us by nominating committee members and helping us spread the word about these standards. These organizations include:

- American Association of Colleges for Teacher Education (AACTE)
- American Association of School Administrators (AASA)
- American Federation of Teachers (AFT)
- Association of Teacher Educators (ATE)
- Council for Exceptional Children (CEC)
- National Association of Elementary School Principals (NAESP)
- National Association for Gifted Children (NAGC)
- National Association of Secondary School Principals (NASSP)
- National Association of State Boards of Education (NASBE)
- National Association of State Directors of Special Education (NASDSE)
- National Association of State Directors of Teacher Education and Certification (NASDTEC)
- National Board for Professional Teaching Standards (NBPTS)
- National Commission on Teaching and America's Future (NCTAF)
- National Council for Accreditation of Teacher Education (NCATE)
- National Education Association (NEA)
- National School Boards Association (NSBA)
- National Teacher of the Year Program
- Teach for America (TFA)
- Teacher Education Accreditation Council (TEAC)

Introduction

The Council of Chief State School Officers (CCSSO), through its Interstate Teacher Assessment and Support Consortium (InTASC), is pleased to offer this set of model core teaching standards that outline what teachers should know and be able to do to ensure every K-12 student reaches the goal of being ready to enter college or the workforce in today's world. These standards outline the common principles and foundations of teaching practice that cut across all subject areas and grade levels and that are necessary to improve student achievement.

More importantly, these Model Core Teaching Standards articulate what effective teaching and learning looks like in a transformed public education system – one that empowers every learner to take ownership of their learning, that emphasizes the learning of content and application of knowledge and skill to real world problems, that values the differences each learner brings to the learning experience, and that leverages rapidly changing learning environments by recognizing the possibilities they bring to maximize learning and engage learners. A transformed public education system requires a new vision of teaching.

A New Vision of Teaching for Improved Student Achievement

The updating of the core teaching standards was driven not only by new understandings of learners and learning but also by the new imperative that every student can and must achieve to high standards. Educators are now being held to new levels of accountability for improved student outcomes. These standards embrace this new emphasis and describe what effective teaching that leads to improved student achievement looks like. They are based on our best understanding of current research on teaching practice with the acknowledgement that how students learn and strategies for engaging learners are evolving more quickly than ever. These standards promote a new paradigm for delivering education and call for a new infrastructure of support for professionals in that system. Below are the key themes that run through the updated teaching standards and how they will drive improved student learning.

> **These standards … describe what effective teaching that leads to improved student achievement looks like.**

Personalized Learning for Diverse Learners

The explosion of learner diversity means teachers need knowledge and skills to customize learning for learners with a range of individual differences. These differences include students who have learning disabilities and students who perform above grade level and deserve opportunities to accelerate. Differences also include cultural and linguistic diversity and the specific needs of students for whom English is a new language. Teachers need to recognize that all learners bring to their learning varying experiences, abilities, talents, and prior learning, as well as language, culture, and family and community values that are assets that can be used to promote their learning. To do this effectively, teachers must have a deeper understanding of their own frames of reference (e.g., culture, gender, language, abilities, ways of knowing), the potential biases in these frames, and their impact on expectations for and relationships with learners and their families.

Finally, teachers need to provide multiple approaches to learning for each student. One aspect of the power of technology is that it has made learners both more independent and more collaborative. The core teaching standards assign learners a more active role in determining what they learn, how they learn it, and how they can demonstrate their learning. They also encourage learners to interact with peers to accomplish their learning goals. In these ways, the standards embody a vision of teaching that personalizes each learner's experiences while ensuring that every learner achieves to high levels.

A Stronger Focus on Application of Knowledge and Skills

Today's learners need both the academic and global skills and knowledge necessary to navigate the world—attributes and dispositions such as problem solving, curiosity, creativity, innovation, communication, interpersonal skills, the ability to synthesize across disciplines, global awareness, ethics, and technological expertise. CCSSO and the National Governors Association are leading the work on articulating what learners need to know and be able to do. The Common Core State Standards for English Language Arts and Mathematics are benchmarked to international standards and include rigorous content and application of knowledge through high-order skills. As states adopt these standards, educators throughout the nation will be reexamining what students should know and be able to do throughout their K–12 education experience.

> **The standards stress that teachers build literacy and thinking skills across the curriculum [and] help learners address multiple perspectives in exploring ideas and solving problems.**

The core teaching standards describe what teachers should know and be able to do in today's learning context to ensure students reach these learning goals. For example, cross-disciplinary skills (e.g., communication, collaboration, critical thinking, and the use of technology) are woven throughout the teaching standards because of their importance for learners. Additionally, the core teaching standards stress that teachers build literacy and thinking skills across the curriculum, as well as help learners address multiple perspectives in exploring ideas and solving problems. The core teaching standards also address interdisciplinary themes (e.g., financial literacy, civic literacy) and the teacher's ability to design learning experiences that draw upon multiple disciplines.

Improved Assessment Literacy

The current education system treats assessment as a function largely separated from teaching. Yet, teachers are expected to use data to improve instruction and support learner success. The core teaching standards recognize that, to meet this expectation, teachers need to have greater knowledge and skill around how to develop a range of assessments, how to balance use of formative and summative assessment as appropriate, and how to use assessment data to understand each learner's progress, adjust instruction as needed, provide feedback to learners, and document learner progress against standards. In addition, teachers need to be prepared to make data-informed decisions at varied levels of assessment, from once-a-year state testing, to district benchmark tests several times a year, to ongoing formative and summative assessments at the classroom-level. This work occurs both independently and collaboratively and involves ongoing learning and reflection.

A Collaborative Professional Culture

Our current system of education tends to isolate teachers and treat teaching as a private act. This is counter to the way we think about teaching today. Just as collaboration among learners improves student learning, we know that collaboration among teachers improves practice. When teachers collectively engage in participatory decision-making, designing lessons, using data, and examining student work, they are able to deliver rigorous and relevant learning for all students and personalize learning for individual students. The core teaching standards require transparency of practice and ongoing, embedded professional learning where teachers engage in collective inquiry. This includes participating actively as a team member in decision-making processes that include building a shared vision and supportive culture, identifying common goals, and monitoring progress toward those goals. It further includes giving and receiving feedback on practice, examining student work, analyzing data from multiple sources, and taking responsibility for each student's learning.

New Leadership Roles for Teachers and Administrators

These core teaching standards set forth new and high expectations for teachers, including around leadership. Integrated across the standards is the teacher's responsibility for the learning of all students, the expectation that they will see themselves as leaders from the beginning of their career and advocate for each student's needs, and the obligation to actively investigate and consider new ideas that will improve teaching and learning and advance the profession. Leadership responsibilities are also implicit as teachers participate in the new collaborative culture. Teachers are expected to work with and share responsibility with colleagues, administrators, and school leaders as they work together to improve student learning and teacher working conditions. This includes actively engaging in efforts to build a shared vision and supportive culture within a school or learning environment, establish mutual expectations and ongoing communication with families, and involve the community in meeting common goals.

> Integrated across the standards is the teacher's responsibility for the learning of all students [and] the expectation that they will see themselves as leaders from the beginning of their career.

Purpose of this Document

The purpose of this document is to serve as a resource for states, districts, professional organizations, teacher education programs, teachers, and others as they develop policies and programs to prepare, license, support, evaluate, and reward today's teachers. As noted above, a systemic approach and supportive infrastructure are essential to successful implementation of these standards. In addition to this standards document, CCSSO has also released a complementary policy discussion document that outlines key considerations, recommendations, and cautions for using the standards to inform policy. This paper builds off of CCSSO's Education Workforce white paper (www.ccsso.org/intasc), which outlines the chiefs' strategic goals in building an educator development and support system of which these standards are the first step.

In updating the InTASC model standards, efforts were made to ensure they align with other national and state standards documents that were recently revised or released. Specifically, this document has been reviewed to ensure compatibility with the recently-released Common Core State Standards for students in mathematics and English language arts, the National Board for Professional Teaching Standards (NBPTS) accomplished teaching core principles, the National Council for Accreditation of Teacher Education (NCATE) accreditation standards, the National Staff Development Council (NSDC) (now called Learning Forward) professional development standards, and the Interstate School Leader Licensure Consortium (ISLLC) 2008 educational leadership policy standards and CCSSO's companion document of performance expectations and indicators for education leaders.

Consistency among all these documents ensures a coherent continuum of expectations for teachers from beginning through accomplished practice, and sets the conditions necessary to support professional growth along this continuum. It also increases the probability of building aligned systems of teacher development and support that begin with recruitment and preparation and run through induction, ongoing professional development, accomplished teaching, and other leadership roles. For a discussion of the implications of these updated standards for teacher policy and practice across the career continuum, please see the companion policy document (www.ccsso.org/intasc).

About These Standards

This document is an update to INTASC's *Model Standards for Beginning Teacher Licensing and Development: A Resource for State Dialogue*, which were released in 1992. These standards differ from the original standards in one key respect: These standards are no longer intended only for "beginning" teachers but as professional practice standards, setting one standard for performance that will look different at different developmental stages of the teacher's career. What distinguishes the beginning from the accomplished teacher is the degree of sophistication in the application of the knowledge and skills. To reflect this change in emphasis, InTASC removed "new" from its name and now is called the Interstate Teacher Assessment and Support Consortium (InTASC).

> **These standards are no longer intended only for "beginning" teachers but as professional practice standards.**

Another key point is that these standards maintain the delineation of knowledge, dispositions, and performances as a way to probe the complexity of the teacher's practice. The relationships among the three have been reframed, however, putting performance first—as the aspect that can be observed and assessed in teaching practice. The others were renamed. "Essential knowledge" signals the role of declarative and procedural knowledge as necessary for effective practice and "critical dispositions" indicates that habits of professional action and moral commitments that underlie the performances play a key role in how teachers do, in fact, act in practice.

Vocabulary choice in the document was deliberate to be consistent with the vision being presented. For example, wherever possible "student" was replaced with "learner" because learner implies an active role in learning whereas student could be seen as more passive. Learner also connotes a more informal and accessible role than that of student. Second, "classroom" was replaced with "learning environment" wherever possible to suggest that learning can occur in any number of contexts and outside of traditional brick and mortar buildings that classroom and school imply.

The reader of these standards should keep in mind that while each standard emphasizes a discrete aspect of teaching, teaching and learning are dynamic, integrated and reciprocal processes. Thus, of necessity, the standards overlap and must be taken as a whole in order to convey a complete picture of the acts of teaching and learning.

> **The indicators are not intended to be a checklist, but rather helpful ways to picture what the standard means.**

Also, it is important to keep in mind that indicators are examples of how a teacher might demonstrate each standard. In a performance assessment of teaching covering several days, one would not expect the teacher to demonstrate every indicator—and there may be other indicators that would provide excellent evidence for the standard that the committee did not set forth here. Thus, the indicators are not intended to be a checklist, but rather helpful ways to picture what the standard means.

Next Steps

Standards can serve three different functions. First, they can serve as a "banner" and lay out a big picture vision of where we want to go. Second, they can define a specific "bar" or level of performance that must be met. Third, they can articulate the "opportunity to learn" supports that must be in place to ensure a teacher candidate has opportunity to meet the standards. All three are essential to success. These Model Core Teaching Standards are the banner in that their purpose is to describe a new vision of teaching to which we aspire as we work to transform our education system to meet the needs of today's learners. It is a reform document designed to help us see and come to consensus on where it is we want to go.

> The purpose [of the standards] is to describe a new vision of teaching to which we aspire as we work to transform our education system to meet the needs of today's learners.

The next step of the work is to take these standards and translate them into a developmental continuum and performance rubrics that can be used to assess performance at key points along the teacher's career. Simultaneously, we must build the infrastructure of accountability and support to match the new vision of teaching. Some of this work has already begun. We look forward to working with states and partners in developing consensus around this common core of teaching and moving these standards into practice.

Resources and Research Behind the Standards

The committee drew upon a range of resources in revising the standards. This included key research literature, the work of states who had already updated their standards, and additional key resources such as books and documents related to 21st century learning.

In addition to the above, the committee members themselves—teachers, teacher educators, researchers, state policy leaders—were selected to assure expertise across a range of topics important to the update process. Their expertise was another key resource in the development of the revised standards.

On the issue of research, InTASC commissioned a review of the literature to capture the current evidence base during the standards-writing process. Periodic research updates were given to the committee as the standards work was under way and additional focus areas were added to the review as the committee identified the key ideas grounding its work. The literature review can be found at the InTASC website (www.ccsso.org/intasc) including summary statements of what we know and where there are gaps are in the research. CCSSO considers the research base a work in progress and seeks feedback on the website.

Summary of Updated InTASC Core Teaching Standards

The standards have been grouped into four general categories to help users organize their thinking about the standards:

The Learner and Learning

Teaching begins with the learner. To ensure that each student learns new knowledge and skills, teachers must understand that learning and developmental patterns vary among individuals, that learners bring unique individual differences to the learning process, and that learners need supportive and safe learning environments to thrive. Effective teachers have high expectations for each and every learner and implement developmentally appropriate, challenging learning experiences within a variety of learning environments that help all learners meet high standards and reach their full potential. Teachers do this by combining a base of professional knowledge, including an understanding of how cognitive, linguistic, social, emotional, and physical development occurs, with the recognition that learners are individuals who bring differing personal and family backgrounds, skills, abilities, perspectives, talents and interests. Teachers collaborate with learners, colleagues, school leaders, families, members of the learners' communities, and community organizations to better understand their students and maximize their learning. Teachers promote learners' acceptance of responsibility for their own learning and collaborate with them to ensure the effective design and implementation of both self-directed and collaborative learning.

> Standard #1: Learner Development. The teacher understands how learners grow and develop, recognizing that patterns of learning and development vary individually within and across the cognitive, linguistic, social, emotional, and physical areas, and designs and implements developmentally appropriate and challenging learning experiences.
>
> Standard #2: Learning Differences. The teacher uses understanding of individual differences and diverse cultures and communities to ensure inclusive learning environments that enable each learner to meet high standards.
>
> Standard #3: Learning Environments. The teacher works with others to create environments that support individual and collaborative learning, and that encourage positive social interaction, active engagement in learning, and self motivation.

Content

Teachers must have a deep and flexible understanding of their content areas and be able to draw upon content knowledge as they work with learners to access information, apply knowledge in real world settings, and address meaningful issues to assure learner mastery of the content. Today's teachers make content knowledge accessible to learners by using multiple means of communication, including digital media and information technology. They integrate cross-disciplinary skills (e.g., critical thinking, problem solving, creativity, communication) to help learners use content to propose solutions, forge new understandings, solve problems, and imagine possibilities. Finally, teachers make content knowledge relevant to learners by connecting it to local, state, national, and global issues.

> Standard #4: Content Knowledge. The teacher understands the central concepts, tools of inquiry, and structures of the discipline(s) he or she teaches and creates learning experiences that make the discipline accessible and meaningful for learners to assure mastery of the content.
>
> Standard #5: Application of Content. The teacher understands how to connect concepts and use differing perspectives to engage learners in critical thinking, creativity, and collaborative problem solving related to authentic local and global issues.

Instructional Practice

Effective instructional practice requires that teachers understand and integrate assessment, planning, and instructional strategies in coordinated and engaging ways. Beginning with their end or goal, teachers first identify student learning objectives and content standards and align assessments to those objectives. Teachers understand how to design, implement and interpret results from a range of formative and summative assessments. This knowledge is integrated into instructional practice so that teachers have access to information that can be used to provide immediate feedback to reinforce student learning and to modify instruction. Planning focuses on using a variety of appropriate and targeted instructional strategies to address diverse ways of learning, to incorporate new technologies to maximize and individualize learning, and to allow learners to take charge of their own learning and do it in creative ways.

> Standard #6: Assessment. The teacher understands and uses multiple methods of assessment to engage learners in their own growth, to monitor learner progress, and to guide the teacher's and learner's decision making.
>
> Standard #7: Planning for Instruction. The teacher plans instruction that supports every student in meeting rigorous learning goals by drawing upon knowledge of content areas, curriculum, cross-disciplinary skills, and pedagogy, as well as knowledge of learners and the community context.
>
> Standard #8: Instructional Strategies. The teacher understands and uses a variety of instructional strategies to encourage learners to develop deep understanding of content areas and their connections, and to build skills to apply knowledge in meaningful ways.

Professional Responsibility

Creating and supporting safe, productive learning environments that result in learners achieving at the highest levels is a teacher's primary responsibility. To do this well, teachers must engage in meaningful and intensive professional learning and self-renewal by regularly examining practice through ongoing study, self-reflection, and collaboration. A cycle of continuous self-improvement is enhanced by leadership, collegial support, and collaboration. Active engagement in professional learning and collaboration results in the discovery and implementation of better practice for the purpose of improved teaching and learning. Teachers also contribute to improving instructional practices that meet learners' needs and accomplish their school's mission and goals. Teachers benefit from and participate in collaboration with learners, families, colleagues, other school professionals, and community members. Teachers demonstrate leadership by modeling ethical behavior, contributing to positive changes in practice, and advancing their profession.

> Standard #9: Professional Learning and Ethical Practice. The teacher engages in ongoing professional learning and uses evidence to continually evaluate his/her practice, particularly the effects of his/her choices and actions on others (learners, families, other professionals, and the community), and adapts practice to meet the needs of each learner.
>
> Standard #10: Leadership and Collaboration. The teacher seeks appropriate leadership roles and opportunities to take responsibility for student learning, to collaborate with learners, families, colleagues, other school professionals, and community members to ensure learner growth, and to advance the profession.

Standard #1: Learner Development

The teacher understands how learners grow and develop, recognizing that patterns of learning and development vary individually within and across the cognitive, linguistic, social, emotional, and physical areas, and designs and implements developmentally appropriate and challenging learning experiences.

PERFORMANCES

1(a) The teacher regularly assesses individual and group performance in order to design and modify instruction to meet learners' needs in each area of development (cognitive, linguistic, social, emotional, and physical) and scaffolds the next level of development.

1(b) The teacher creates developmentally appropriate instruction that takes into account individual learners' strengths, interests, and needs and that enables each learner to advance and accelerate his/her learning.

1(c) The teacher collaborates with families, communities, colleagues, and other professionals to promote learner growth and development.

ESSENTIAL KNOWLEDGE

1(d) The teacher understands how learning occurs-- how learners construct knowledge, acquire skills, and develop disciplined thinking processes--and knows how to use instructional strategies that promote student learning.

1(e) The teacher understands that each learner's cognitive, linguistic, social, emotional, and physical development influences learning and knows how to make instructional decisions that build on learners' strengths and needs.

1(f) The teacher identifies readiness for learning, and understands how development in any one area may affect performance in others.

1(g) The teacher understands the role of language and culture in learning and knows how to modify instruction to make language comprehensible and instruction relevant, accessible, and challenging.

CRITICAL DISPOSITIONS

1(h) The teacher respects learners' differing strengths and needs and is committed to using this information to further each learner's development.

1(i) The teacher is committed to using learners' strengths as a basis for growth, and their misconceptions as opportunities for learning.

1(j) The teacher takes responsibility for promoting learners' growth and development.

1(k) The teacher values the input and contributions of families, colleagues, and other professionals in understanding and supporting each learner's development.

Standard #2: Learning Differences

The teacher uses understanding of individual differences and diverse cultures and communities to ensure inclusive learning environments that enable each learner to meet high standards.

PERFORMANCES

2(a) The teacher designs, adapts, and delivers instruction to address each student's diverse learning strengths and needs and creates opportunities for students to demonstrate their learning in different ways.

2(b) The teacher makes appropriate and timely provisions (e.g., pacing for individual rates of growth, task demands, communication, assessment, and response modes) for individual students with particular learning differences or needs.

2(c) The teacher designs instruction to build on learners' prior knowledge and experiences, allowing learners to accelerate as they demonstrate their understandings.

2(d) The teacher brings multiple perspectives to the discussion of content, including attention to learners' personal, family, and community experiences and cultural norms.

2(e) The teacher incorporates tools of language development into planning and instruction, including strategies for making content accessible to English language learners and for evaluating and supporting their development of English proficiency.

2(f) The teacher accesses resources, supports, and specialized assistance and services to meet particular learning differences or needs.

ESSENTIAL KNOWLEDGE

2(g) The teacher understands and identifies differences in approaches to learning and performance and knows how to design instruction that uses each learner's strengths to promote growth.

2(h) The teacher understands students with exceptional needs, including those associated with disabilities and giftedness, and knows how to use strategies and resources to address these needs.

2(i) The teacher knows about second language acquisition processes and knows how to incorporate instructional strategies and resources to support language acquisition.

2(j) The teacher understands that learners bring assets for learning based on their individual experiences, abilities, talents, prior learning, and peer and social group interactions, as well as language, culture, family, and community values.

2(k) The teacher knows how to access information about the values of diverse cultures and communities and how to incorporate learners' experiences, cultures, and community resources into instruction.

CRITICAL DISPOSITIONS

2(l) The teacher believes that all learners can achieve at high levels and persists in helping each learner reach his/her full potential.

2(m) The teacher respects learners as individuals with differing personal and family backgrounds and various skills, abilities, perspectives, talents, and interests.

2(n) The teacher makes learners feel valued and helps them learn to value each other.

2(o) The teacher values diverse languages and dialects and seeks to integrate them into his/her instructional practice to engage students in learning.

Standard #3: Learning Environments

The teacher works with others to create environments that support individual and collaborative learning, and that encourage positive social interaction, active engagement in learning, and self motivation.

PERFORMANCES

3(a) The teacher collaborates with learners, families, and colleagues to build a safe, positive learning climate of openness, mutual respect, support, and inquiry.

3(b) The teacher develops learning experiences that engage learners in collaborative and self-directed learning and that extend learner interaction with ideas and people locally and globally.

3(c) The teacher collaborates with learners and colleagues to develop shared values and expectations for respectful interactions, rigorous academic discussions, and individual and group responsibility for quality work.

3(d) The teacher manages the learning environment to actively and equitably engage learners by organizing, allocating, and coordinating the resources of time, space, and learners' attention.

3(e) The teacher uses a variety of methods to engage learners in evaluating the learning environment and collaborates with learners to make appropriate adjustments.

3(f) The teacher communicates verbally and nonverbally in ways that demonstrate respect for and responsiveness to the cultural backgrounds and differing perspectives learners bring to the learning environment.

3(g) The teacher promotes responsible learner use of interactive technologies to extend the possibilities for learning locally and globally.

3(h) The teacher intentionally builds learner capacity to collaborate in face-to-face and virtual environments through applying effective interpersonal communication skills.

ESSENTIAL KNOWLEDGE

3(i) The teacher understands the relationship between motivation and engagement and knows how to design learning experiences using strategies that build learner self-direction and ownership of learning.

3(j) The teacher knows how to help learners work productively and cooperatively with each other to achieve learning goals.

3(k) The teacher knows how to collaborate with learners to establish and monitor elements of a safe and productive learning environment including norms, expectations, routines, and organizational structures.

3(l) The teacher understands how learner diversity can affect communication and knows how to communicate effectively in differing environments.

3(m) The teacher knows how to use technologies and how to guide learners to apply them in appropriate, safe, and effective ways.

CRITICAL DISPOSITIONS

3(n) The teacher is committed to working with learners, colleagues, families, and communities to establish positive and supportive learning environments.

3(o) The teacher values the role of learners in promoting each other's learning and recognizes the importance of peer relationships in establishing a climate of learning.

3(p) The teacher is committed to supporting learners as they participate in decision making, engage in exploration and invention, work collaboratively and independently, and engage in purposeful learning.

3(q) The teacher seeks to foster respectful communication among all members of the learning community.

3(r) The teacher is a thoughtful and responsive listener and observer.

Standard #4: Content Knowledge

The teacher understands the central concepts, tools of inquiry, and structures of the discipline(s) he or she teaches and creates learning experiences that make these aspects of the discipline accessible and meaningful for learners to assure mastery of the content.

PERFORMANCES

4(a) The teacher effectively uses multiple representations and explanations that capture key ideas in the discipline, guide learners through learning progressions, and promote each learner's achievement of content standards.

4(b) The teacher engages students in learning experiences in the discipline(s) that encourage learners to understand, question, and analyze ideas from diverse perspectives so that they master the content.

4(c) The teacher engages learners in applying methods of inquiry and standards of evidence used in the discipline.

4(d) The teacher stimulates learner reflection on prior content knowledge, links new concepts to familiar concepts, and makes connections to learners' experiences.

4(e) The teacher recognizes learner misconceptions in a discipline that interfere with learning, and creates experiences to build accurate conceptual understanding.

4(f) The teacher evaluates and modifies instructional resources and curriculum materials for their comprehensiveness, accuracy for representing particular concepts in the discipline, and appropriateness for his/her learners.

4(g) The teacher uses supplementary resources and technologies effectively to ensure accessibility and relevance for all learners.

4(h) The teacher creates opportunities for students to learn, practice, and master academic language in their content.

4(i) The teacher accesses school and/or district-based resources to evaluate the learner's content knowledge in their primary language.

ESSENTIAL KNOWLEDGE

4(j) The teacher understands major concepts, assumptions, debates, processes of inquiry, and ways of knowing that are central to the discipline(s) s/he teaches.

4(k) The teacher understands common misconceptions in learning the discipline and how to guide learners to accurate conceptual understanding.

4(l) The teacher knows and uses the academic language of the discipline and knows how to make it accessible to learners.

4(m) The teacher knows how to integrate culturally relevant content to build on learners' background knowledge.

4(n) The teacher has a deep knowledge of student content standards and learning progressions in the discipline(s) s/he teaches.

CRITICAL DISPOSITIONS

4(o) The teacher realizes that content knowledge is not a fixed body of facts but is complex, culturally situated, and ever evolving. S/he keeps abreast of new ideas and understandings in the field.

4(p) The teacher appreciates multiple perspectives within the discipline and facilitates learners' critical analysis of these perspectives.

4(q) The teacher recognizes the potential of bias in his/her representation of the discipline and seeks to appropriately address problems of bias.

4(r) The teacher is committed to work toward each learner's mastery of disciplinary content and skills.

Standard #5: Application of Content

The teacher understands how to connect concepts and use differing perspectives to engage learners in critical thinking, creativity, and collaborative problem solving related to authentic local and global issues.

PERFORMANCES

5(a) The teacher develops and implements projects that guide learners in analyzing the complexities of an issue or question using perspectives from varied disciplines and cross-disciplinary skills (e.g., a water quality study that draws upon biology and chemistry to look at factual information and social studies to examine policy implications).

5(b) The teacher engages learners in applying content knowledge to real world problems through the lens of interdisciplinary themes (e.g., financial literacy, environmental literacy).

5(c) The teacher facilitates learners' use of current tools and resources to maximize content learning in varied contexts.

5(d) The teacher engages learners in questioning and challenging assumptions and approaches in order to foster innovation and problem solving in local and global contexts.

5(e) The teacher develops learners' communication skills in disciplinary and interdisciplinary contexts by creating meaningful opportunities to employ a variety of forms of communication that address varied audiences and purposes.

5(f) The teacher engages learners in generating and evaluating new ideas and novel approaches, seeking inventive solutions to problems, and developing original work.

5(g) The teacher facilitates learners' ability to develop diverse social and cultural perspectives that expand their understanding of local and global issues and create novel approaches to solving problems.

5(h) The teacher develops and implements supports for learner literacy development across content areas.

ESSENTIAL KNOWLEDGE

5(i) The teacher understands the ways of knowing in his/her discipline, how it relates to other disciplinary approaches to inquiry, and the strengths and limitations of each approach in addressing problems, issues, and concerns.

5(j) The teacher understands how current interdisciplinary themes (e.g., civic literacy, health literacy, global awareness) connect to the core subjects and knows how to weave those themes into meaningful learning experiences.

5(k) The teacher understands the demands of accessing and managing information as well as how to evaluate issues of ethics and quality related to information and its use.

5(l) The teacher understands how to use digital and interactive technologies for efficiently and effectively achieving specific learning goals.

5(m) The teacher understands critical thinking processes and knows how to help learners develop high level questioning skills to promote their independent learning.

5(n) The teacher understands communication modes and skills as vehicles for learning (e.g., information gathering and processing) across disciplines as well as vehicles for expressing learning.

5(o) The teacher understands creative thinking processes and how to engage learners in producing original work.

5(p) The teacher knows where and how to access resources to build global awareness and understanding, and how to integrate them into the curriculum.

CRITICAL DISPOSITIONS

5(q) The teacher is constantly exploring how to use disciplinary knowledge as a lens to address local and global issues.

5(r) The teacher values knowledge outside his/her own content area and how such knowledge enhances student learning.

5(s) The teacher values flexible learning environments that encourage learner exploration, discovery, and expression across content areas.

Standard #6: Assessment

The teacher understands and uses multiple methods of assessment to engage learners in their own growth, to monitor learner progress, and to guide the teacher's and learner's decision making.

PERFORMANCES

6(a) The teacher balances the use of formative and summative assessment as appropriate to support, verify, and document learning.

6(b) The teacher designs assessments that match learning objectives with assessment methods and minimizes sources of bias that can distort assessment results.

6(c) The teacher works independently and collaboratively to examine test and other performance data to understand each learner's progress and to guide planning.

6(d) The teacher engages learners in understanding and identifying quality work and provides them with effective descriptive feedback to guide their progress toward that work.

6(e) The teacher engages learners in multiple ways of demonstrating knowledge and skill as part of the assessment process.

6(f) The teacher models and structures processes that guide learners in examining their own thinking and learning as well as the performance of others.

6(g) The teacher effectively uses multiple and appropriate types of assessment data to identify each student's learning needs and to develop differentiated learning experiences.

6(h) The teacher prepares all learners for the demands of particular assessment formats and makes appropriate accommodations in assessments or testing conditions, especially for learners with disabilities and language learning needs.

6(i) The teacher continually seeks appropriate ways to employ technology to support assessment practice both to engage learners more fully and to assess and address learner needs.

ESSENTIAL KNOWLEDGE

6(j) The teacher understands the differences between formative and summative applications of assessment and knows how and when to use each.

6(k) The teacher understands the range of types and multiple purposes of assessment and how to design, adapt, or select appropriate assessments to address specific learning goals and individual differences, and to minimize sources of bias.

6(l) The teacher knows how to analyze assessment data to understand patterns and gaps in learning, to guide planning and instruction, and to provide meaningful feedback to all learners.

6(m) The teacher knows when and how to engage learners in analyzing their own assessment results and in helping to set goals for their own learning.

6(n) The teacher understands the positive impact of effective descriptive feedback for learners and knows a variety of strategies for communicating this feedback.

6(o) The teacher knows when and how to evaluate and report learner progress against standards.

6(p) The teacher understands how to prepare learners for assessments and how to make accommodations in assessments and testing conditions, especially for learners with disabilities and language learning needs.

CRITICAL DISPOSITIONS

6(q) The teacher is committed to engaging learners actively in assessment processes and to developing each learner's capacity to review and communicate about their own progress and learning.

6(r) The teacher takes responsibility for aligning instruction and assessment with learning goals.

6(s) The teacher is committed to providing timely and effective descriptive feedback to learners on their progress.

6(t) The teacher is committed to using multiple types of assessment processes to support, verify, and document learning.

6(u) The teacher is committed to making accommodations in assessments and testing conditions, especially for learners with disabilities and language learning needs.

6(v) The teacher is committed to the ethical use of various assessments and assessment data to identify learner strengths and needs to promote learner growth.

Standard #7: Planning for Instruction

The teacher plans instruction that supports every student in meeting rigorous learning goals by drawing upon knowledge of content areas, curriculum, cross-disciplinary skills, and pedagogy, as well as knowledge of learners and the community context.

PERFORMANCES

7(a) The teacher individually and collaboratively selects and creates learning experiences that are appropriate for curriculum goals and content standards, and are relevant to learners.

7(b) The teacher plans how to achieve each student's learning goals, choosing appropriate strategies and accommodations, resources, and materials to differentiate instruction for individuals and groups of learners.

7(c) The teacher develops appropriate sequencing of learning experiences and provides multiple ways to demonstrate knowledge and skill.

7(d) The teacher plans for instruction based on formative and summative assessment data, prior learner knowledge, and learner interest.

7(e) The teacher plans collaboratively with professionals who have specialized expertise (e.g., special educators, related service providers, language learning specialists, librarians, media specialists) to design and jointly deliver as appropriate learning experiences to meet unique learning needs.

7(f) The teacher evaluates plans in relation to short- and long-range goals and systematically adjusts plans to meet each student's learning needs and enhance learning.

ESSENTIAL KNOWLEDGE

7(g) The teacher understands content and content standards and how these are organized in the curriculum.

7(h) The teacher understands how integrating cross-disciplinary skills in instruction engages learners purposefully in applying content knowledge.

7(i) The teacher understands learning theory, human development, cultural diversity, and individual differences and how these impact ongoing planning.

7(j) The teacher understands the strengths and needs of individual learners and how to plan instruction that is responsive to these strengths and needs.

7(k) The teacher knows a range of evidence-based instructional strategies, resources, and technological tools and how to use them effectively to plan instruction that meets diverse learning needs.

7(l) The teacher knows when and how to adjust plans based on assessment information and learner responses.

7(m) The teacher knows when and how to access resources and collaborate with others to support student learning (e.g., special educators, related service providers, language learner specialists, librarians, media specialists, community organizations).

CRITICAL DISPOSITIONS

7(n) The teacher respects learners' diverse strengths and needs and is committed to using this information to plan effective instruction.

7(o) The teacher values planning as a collegial activity that takes into consideration the input of learners, colleagues, families, and the larger community.

7(p) The teacher takes professional responsibility to use short- and long-term planning as a means of assuring student learning.

7(q) The teacher believes that plans must always be open to adjustment and revision based on learner needs and changing circumstances.

Standard #8: Instructional Strategies

The teacher understands and uses a variety of instructional strategies to encourage learners to develop deep understanding of content areas and their connections, and to build skills to apply knowledge in meaningful ways.

PERFORMANCES

8(a) The teacher uses appropriate strategies and resources to adapt instruction to the needs of individuals and groups of learners.

8(b) The teacher continuously monitors student learning, engages learners in assessing their progress, and adjusts instruction in response to student learning needs.

8(c) The teacher collaborates with learners to design and implement relevant learning experiences, identify their strengths, and access family and community resources to develop their areas of interest.

8(d) The teacher varies his/her role in the instructional process (e.g., instructor, facilitator, coach, audience) in relation to the content and purposes of instruction and the needs of learners.

8(e) The teacher provides multiple models and representations of concepts and skills with opportunities for learners to demonstrate their knowledge through a variety of products and performances.

8(f) The teacher engages all learners in developing higher order questioning skills and metacognitive processes.

8(g) The teacher engages learners in using a range of learning skills and technology tools to access, interpret, evaluate, and apply information.

8(h) The teacher uses a variety of instructional strategies to support and expand learners' communication through speaking, listening, reading, writing, and other modes.

8(i) The teacher asks questions to stimulate discussion that serves different purposes (e.g., probing for learner understanding, helping learners articulate their ideas and thinking processes, stimulating curiosity, and helping learners to question).

ESSENTIAL KNOWLEDGE

8(j) The teacher understands the cognitive processes associated with various kinds of learning (e.g., critical and creative thinking, problem framing and problem solving, invention, memorization and recall) and how these processes can be stimulated.

8(k) The teacher knows how to apply a range of developmentally, culturally, and linguistically appropriate instructional strategies to achieve learning goals.

8(l) The teacher knows when and how to use appropriate strategies to differentiate instruction and engage all learners in complex thinking and meaningful tasks.

8(m) The teacher understands how multiple forms of communication (oral, written, nonverbal, digital, visual) convey ideas, foster self expression, and build relationships.

8(n) The teacher knows how to use a wide variety of resources, including human and technological, to engage students in learning.

8(o) The teacher understands how content and skill development can be supported by media and technology and knows how to evaluate these resources for quality, accuracy, and effectiveness.

CRITICAL DISPOSITIONS

8(p) The teacher is committed to deepening awareness and understanding the strengths and needs of diverse learners when planning and adjusting instruction.

8(q) The teacher values the variety of ways people communicate and encourages learners to develop and use multiple forms of communication.

8(r) The teacher is committed to exploring how the use of new and emerging technologies can support and promote student learning.

8(s) The teacher values flexibility and reciprocity in the teaching process as necessary for adapting instruction to learner responses, ideas, and needs.

Standard #9: Professional Learning and Ethical Practice

The teacher engages in ongoing professional learning and uses evidence to continually evaluate his/her practice, particularly the effects of his/her choices and actions on others (learners, families, other professionals, and the community), and adapts practice to meet the needs of each learner.

PERFORMANCES

9(a) The teacher engages in ongoing learning opportunities to develop knowledge and skills in order to provide all learners with engaging curriculum and learning experiences based on local and state standards.

9(b) The teacher engages in meaningful and appropriate professional learning experiences aligned with his/her own needs and the needs of the learners, school, and system.

9(c) Independently and in collaboration with colleagues, the teacher uses a variety of data (e.g., systematic observation, information about learners, research) to evaluate the outcomes of teaching and learning and to adapt planning and practice.

9(d) The teacher actively seeks professional, community, and technological resources, within and outside the school, as supports for analysis, reflection, and problem-solving.

9(e) The teacher reflects on his/her personal biases and accesses resources to deepen his/her own understanding of cultural, ethnic, gender, and learning differences to build stronger relationships and create more relevant learning experiences.

9(f) The teacher advocates, models, and teaches safe, legal, and ethical use of information and technology including appropriate documentation of sources and respect for others in the use of social media.

ESSENTIAL KNOWLEDGE

9(g) The teacher understands and knows how to use a variety of self-assessment and problem-solving strategies to analyze and reflect on his/her practice and to plan for adaptations/adjustments.

9(h) The teacher knows how to use learner data to analyze practice and differentiate instruction accordingly.

9(i) The teacher understands how personal identity, worldview, and prior experience affect perceptions and expectations, and recognizes how they may bias behaviors and interactions with others.

9(j) The teacher understands laws related to learners' rights and teacher responsibilities (e.g., for educational equity, appropriate education for learners with disabilities, confidentiality, privacy, appropriate treatment of learners, reporting in situations related to possible child abuse).

9(k) The teacher knows how to build and implement a plan for professional growth directly aligned with his/her needs as a growing professional using feedback from teacher evaluations and observations, data on learner performance, and school- and system-wide priorities.

CRITICAL DISPOSITIONS

9(l) The teacher takes responsibility for student learning and uses ongoing analysis and reflection to improve planning and practice.

9(m) The teacher is committed to deepening understanding of his/her own frames of reference (e.g., culture, gender, language, abilities, ways of knowing), the potential biases in these frames, and their impact on expectations for and relationships with learners and their families.

9(n) The teacher sees him/herself as a learner, continuously seeking opportunities to draw upon current education policy and research as sources of analysis and reflection to improve practice.

9(o) The teacher understands the expectations of the profession including codes of ethics, professional standards of practice, and relevant law and policy.

Standard #10: Leadership and Collaboration

The teacher seeks appropriate leadership roles and opportunities to take responsibility for student learning, to collaborate with learners, families, colleagues, other school professionals, and community members to ensure learner growth, and to advance the profession.

PERFORMANCES

10(a) The teacher takes an active role on the instructional team, giving and receiving feedback on practice, examining learner work, analyzing data from multiple sources, and sharing responsibility for decision making and accountability for each student's learning.

10(b) The teacher works with other school professionals to plan and jointly facilitate learning on how to meet diverse needs of learners.

10(c) The teacher engages collaboratively in the school-wide effort to build a shared vision and supportive culture, identify common goals, and monitor and evaluate progress toward those goals.

10(d) The teacher works collaboratively with learners and their families to establish mutual expectations and ongoing communication to support learner development and achievement.

10(e) Working with school colleagues, the teacher builds ongoing connections with community resources to enhance student learning and well being.

10(f) The teacher engages in professional learning, contributes to the knowledge and skill of others, and works collaboratively to advance professional practice.

10(g) The teacher uses technological tools and a variety of communication strategies to build local and global learning communities that engage learners, families, and colleagues.

10(h) The teacher uses and generates meaningful research on education issues and policies.

10(i) The teacher seeks appropriate opportunities to model effective practice for colleagues, to lead professional learning activities, and to serve in other leadership roles.

10(j) The teacher advocates to meet the needs of learners, to strengthen the learning environment, and to enact system change.

10(k) The teacher takes on leadership roles at the school, district, state, and/or national level and advocates for learners, the school, the community, and the profession.

ESSENTIAL KNOWLEDGE

10(l) The teacher understands schools as organizations within a historical, cultural, political, and social context and knows how to work with others across the system to support learners.

10(m) The teacher understands that alignment of family, school, and community spheres of influence enhances student learning and that discontinuity in these spheres of influence interferes with learning.

10(n) The teacher knows how to work with other adults and has developed skills in collaborative interaction appropriate for both face-to-face and virtual contexts.

10(o) The teacher knows how to contribute to a common culture that supports high expectations for student learning.

CRITICAL DISPOSITIONS

10(p) The teacher actively shares responsibility for shaping and supporting the mission of his/her school as one of advocacy for learners and accountability for their success.

10(q) The teacher respects families' beliefs, norms, and expectations and seeks to work collaboratively with learners and families in setting and meeting challenging goals.

10(r) The teacher takes initiative to grow and develop with colleagues through interactions that enhance practice and support student learning.

10(s) The teacher takes responsibility for contributing to and advancing the profession.

10(t) The teacher embraces the challenge of continuous improvement and change.

Glossary of Terms

This glossary includes only those terms that are helpful to understanding how the InTASC standards have changed, particularly where new emphases or new understandings are implicated.

Academic Language
Academic language, tied to specific subject area disciplines, captures—through vocabulary, grammar, and organizational strategies—the complex ideas, higher order thinking processes, and abstract concepts of the discipline. It is the language used in classrooms, textbooks, and formal presentations in a subject area and differs in structure and vocabulary from everyday spoken English.

Assessment
Assessment is the productive process of monitoring, measuring, evaluating, documenting, reflecting on, and adjusting teaching and learning to ensure students reach high levels of achievement. Assessment systems need to include both formative and summative assessment processes, aligned with instructional and curricular goals and objectives. Formative assessment findings should be used as a continuous feedback loop to improve teaching and learning. Summative assessment results should be used to make final decisions about gains in knowledge and skills.

Formative Assessment
Formative assessment is a process used by teachers and learners that provides a continuous stream of evidence of learner growth, empowering teachers to adjust instruction and learners to adjust learning to improve student achievement. Formative assessment requires clear articulation and communication of intended instructional outcomes and criteria for success, ongoing descriptive feedback, the use of assessment evidence to make adjustments to teaching and learning, self- and peer-assessment that promote learner awareness of growth and needed improvement, and a partnership between teachers and learners that holds both parties accountable for learner achievement and success.

Summative Assessment
Summative assessment is the process of certifying learning at the culmination of a given period of time to evaluate the extent to which instructional objectives have been met. Examples of summative assessment include end-of-unit tests, final exams, semester exams, portfolios, capstone projects, performance demonstrations, state-mandated tests, the National Assessment of Educational Progress (NAEP), and accountability measures (e.g., Adequate Yearly Progress or AYP).

Collaboration
Collaboration is a style of interaction between individuals engaged in shared decision making as they work toward a common goal. Individuals who collaborate have equally valued personal or professional resources to contribute and they share decision-making authority and accountability for outcomes.

Content Knowledge
Content knowledge includes not only a particular set of information, but also the framework for organizing information and processes for working with it. The traditional definition of content knowledge has been extended in these standards in three ways. First, it incorporates the notion of "pedagogical content knowledge," which blends content and effective instructional strategies for teaching particular subject matter, including appropriate representations and explanations. Second, it includes connections to other disciplines and the development of new, interdisciplinary areas of focus such as civic literacy, environmental literacy, and global awareness. Third, the notion of content knowledge is further extended to include cross-disciplinary skills as tools of inquiry and means to probe content deeply and apply it in real world contexts.

Cross-disciplinary Skills

Cross-disciplinary skills 1) allow learners to probe content deeply (e.g., reading comprehension, critical thinking), 2) connect academic disciplines to one another (e.g., problem solving), 3) can be applied to and may be used differently within various fields (e.g., critical thinking in biology vs. critical thinking in literary analysis), and 4) should be taught explicitly in the context of a given content area (e.g., accessing and interpreting information). These skills include critical thinking, problem solving, collaboration, effective oral and written communication, accessing and analyzing information, as well as adaptability, creativity, initiative, and entrepreneurialism.

Cultural Relevance

Cultural relevance is evident through the integration of cultural knowledge, prior experiences, and performance styles of diverse learners to make learning more appropriate and effective for them; it teaches to and through the strengths of these learners. Culturally relevant instruction integrates a wide variety of instructional strategies that are connected to different approaches to learning.

Data and Use of Data

Learner data are factual, evidentiary forms of information about individuals or groups of learners that are collected, documented, organized, and analyzed for the purpose of making decisions about teaching and learning. Examples of learner data include, but are not limited to 1) learner demographics and background information, 2) documented information about learning needs and prior performance, 3) learner class work, homework, and other formal and informal works produced by the learner, 4) progress charts, records, and anecdotal teacher notes from formative assessments and/or classroom observations, 5) end-of-unit teacher-developed tests or summative performances and course grades, and 6) external test scores.

Using data in instructional decision making is a continuous, cyclical process of making instructional decisions based on the analysis of learner data. Using data to inform instructional decisions involves key processes—assessing, analyzing, planning, implementing, and reflecting. Data-informed instructional decision making uses data from multiple sources to understand learning strengths and needs in order to suggest classroom and school-wide instructional solutions. This same cyclical process can be applied to larger education decisions affecting school climate and school improvement efforts, with expanded sets of data that may include, for example, teacher evaluation and professional development, parental involvement, and resource allocation.

Diverse Learners and Learning Differences

Diverse learners and students with learning differences are those who, because of gender, language, cultural background, differing ability levels, disabilities, learning approaches, and/or socioeconomic status may have academic needs that require varied instructional strategies to ensure their learning. Learning differences are manifested in such areas as differing rates of learning, motivation, attention, preferred learning modalities, complexity of reasoning, persistence, foundational knowledge and skills, and preferred learning and response modes.

Diversity

Diversity is inclusive of individual differences (e.g., personality, interests, learning modalities, and life experiences), and group differences (e.g., race, ethnicity, ability, gender identity, gender expression, sexual orientation, nationality, language, religion, political affiliation, and socio-economic background).

Inclusive Learning Environment

Inclusive learning environments are welcoming and accepting of each and every learner including those who are vulnerable to marginalization and exclusion and those who traditionally have been left out or excluded from appropriate educational and learning opportunities. Inclusion incorporates and expands the concept of inclusion that is most frequently associated with the goal of equal access to general education for students with disabilities. Inclusive approaches embrace diversity; provide access to high-level knowledge, skills, and application for every student; adapt instruction to meet individual needs; encourage co-teaching and collaboration among general and resource educators; foster collaboration with families and community members; maintain high expectations of all students; and support student achievement and growth.

Leadership
Leadership in this document refers to attributes of the teacher that include but are not limited to: 1) a view of the teacher's role in education as multifaceted; 2) a keen sense of ethical responsibility to advance the profession while simultaneously advancing knowledge, skills, and opportunities for each learner; 3) a deep commitment to teaching that includes a willingness to actively engage in professional development to expand knowledge about teaching and learning; 4) a willingness to take on the mantle of leadership in the classroom and among colleagues without a formal title; 5) a recognition of when to lead and when it is appropriate to allow others to lead; 6) knowledge of when and how to marshal a variety of stakeholders to work toward a common cause; 7) an ability to regularly garner resources, both human and other, for the betterment of the students and the school; and 8) the ability to make sound decisions based on the appropriate use and interpretation of quality data and evidence. Teacher leaders function well in professional communities, contribute to school improvement, and inspire their students and colleagues to excellence.

Learning Environment
A learning environment is a complex setting designed to attend to the learner(s), the context, and the content simultaneously. Regardless of the setting—whether traditional classroom, community-based, virtual, or other alternative format—a learning environment must motivate student learning through establishing interest, providing choices, making relevant connections, building understanding, assessing learning outcomes, developing close teacher-learner relationships, and creating a sense of belonging between and among learners. Learning environments can be created in varied settings, and the traditional classroom environment itself can be stretched to become more experiential and technology-rich. Technology can engage learners with experts and fellow learners around the world, providing access to authentic problems and real-world applications The development of technology-enriched learning environments can enable learners to pursue their individual curiosities and become active participants in setting their own educational goals, managing their own learning, and assessing their own progress.

Learning Progressions
Learning progressions are descriptions of increasingly sophisticated ways of thinking about a topic and have been proposed as solutions to such educational problems as a lack of curricular coherence, developmental inappropriateness of curricula, misalignment between instruction and assessment, and weaknesses in support for valued teaching practices. They can support teachers' formative assessment practices and help teachers use learners' prior knowledge in productive ways. By laying out the territory that learners are likely to traverse in coming to understand a given concept, these tools can help teachers recognize their learners' misconceptions as productive steps on the way to full understanding.

Professional Development and Professional Learning
Professional development provides comprehensive, sustained, and intensive learning opportunities to expand the professional knowledge base available to teachers and to engage them in an ongoing process of critically examining their teaching practices to find new and more effective ways to improve student learning. Professional development needs to address both an individual teacher's goals for professional growth and the larger organizational learning priorities for school improvement. Professional learning engages teachers in working with others to deepen their content knowledge, sharpen their instructional skills, and develop their ability to use data for meaningful decision making. Thus, professional learning is an ongoing, job-embedded process that supports transfer of newly-learned knowledge and skills to practice. Such learning also needs to be continuously evaluated and refined.

Reference Chart of Key Cross-Cutting Themes in Updated InTASC Standards

This chart shows where in the text of the standards certain key themes are referenced, demonstrating how they have been integrated across the document. In some instances, the key theme is not explicit but can be inferred.

Theme	Knowledge	Disposition	Performance
*Collaboration	3(j), 3(k), 3(i), 5(p), 7(m), 10(l), 10(n)	1(k), 3(n), 3(o), 3(p), 6(q), 6(s), 7(o), 9(l), 10(q), 10(r)	1(c), 3(a), 3(b), 3(c), 3(e), 3(h), 6(c), 7(a), 7(e), 8(b), 8(c), 9(a-d), 10(a-g)
*Communication	3(l), 3(j), 5(n), 6(l), 6(n), 6(o), 8(m), 10(n)	3(q), 3(r), 6(q), 6(s), 8(q)	3(c), 3(e), 3(f), 3(h), 5(e), 6(d), 6(e), 8(h), 8(i), 10(g)
*Creativity/Innovation	5(l), 5(o), 8(j), 8(m)	3(p), 5(s)	5(d), 5(f), 5(g), 8(i), 9(f)
*Critical thinking, problem solving	4(j), 4(k), 4(l), 5(i), 5(m), 8(j), 8(l), 9(g)	4(p), 4(r), 5(q)	4(b), 4(c), 4(d), 4(e), 4(h), 5(a), 5(b), 5(d), 5(f), 5(g), 6(f), 8(f), 8(g), 8(i), 9(d)
Cultural competence	1(g), 2(g), 2(j), 2(k), 3(i), 4(k), 4(m), 7(i), 8(k), 9(i)	4(o), 8(t), 9(m)	2(d), 3(f), 5(h), 7(c), 9(e)
English language learners	1(g), 2(i), 2(j), 6(p), 7(m), 8(m)	2(o), 6(u)	2(d), 2(e), 4(i), 6(h), 7(e)
Families/Communities	2(j), 2(k), 10(m)	1(k), 2(m), 3(n), 7(o), 9(m), 10(q)	1(c), 2(d), 3(a), 8(c), 9(b), 10(c), 10(d), 10(e), 10(g), 10(k)
Individual differences	1(d-g), 2(g), 2(h), 2(j), 2(k), 3(l), 4(l), 4(m), 6(k), 6(l), 6(m), 6(o), 6(p), 7(i-m), 8(k), 8(l), 9(g), 9(h), 9(i), 9(j)	1(h), 1(i), 1(k), 2(l), 2(m), 2(n), 2(o), 4(r), 6(q), 6(s), 6(u), 7(n), 7(q), 8(p), 8(s), 9(m)	1(a), 1(b), 2(a-f), 2(h), 3(d), 3(f), 4(a), 4(d), 4(e), 4(f), 4(g), 6(c), 6(d), 6(g), 6(h), 6(i), 7(b), 7(c), 7(d-f), 8(a), 8(b), 8(d), 8(e), 8(f), 9(a), 9(c), 9(e), 10(a). 10(b)
Interdisciplinary themes	5(j)	5(q-s)	5(c), 5(b), 5(e)
Leadership	1(c), 3(k), 5(p), 7(l), 7(m), 8(l), 8(n), 9(i), 9(j), 10(l-o)	1(j), 3(n), 4(p), 5(q), 6(r), 6(v), 7(o), 7(p), 8(s), 9(m), 9(n), 10(p-t)	2(f), 3(a), 3(c), 3(d), 4(g), 5(d), 5(g), 6(c), 6(e), 6(f), 7(a), 7(e), 8(c), 8(d), 9(a-f), 10(a-k)
*Multiple perspectives	5(i), 5(j), 5(n), 5(p), 9(i), 7(h), 10(l), 10(m)	4(p), 5(r), 6(t)	2(d), 3(e), 4(b), 5(a), 5(b), 5(d), 5(e), 5(g)
Professional learning	6(j-p), 7(f), 7(k), 8(k), 8(n), 8(o), 9(g-k)	4(o), 4(p), 4(q), 5(q), 5(r), 6(t), 8(p), 9(l-o), 10(r), 10(s), 10(t)	6(a), 6(c), 6(g), 6(i), 8(g), 9(a-f), 10(f), 10(h)
Student-directed learning	3(i), 3(k), 5(m), 6(m)	3(n), 3(o), 3(p), 6(q), 6(s), 10(q)	3(b), 3(c), 5(d), 5(f), 6(f), 8(b), 8(c)
Teacher responsibility	3(m), 5(l), 9(j), 9(k), 10(o)	1(j), 4(o), 4(q), 5(r), 6(r), 6(t), 6(u), 6(v), 7(p), 9(l-o), 10(p), 10(r), 10(s)	3(c), 3(g), 5(h), 9(e), 9(f)
*Technology	3(j), 3(m), 5(k), 5(l), 7(k), 8(n), 8(o), 10(n)	8(q), 8(r)	3(g), 3(h), 4(g), 5(c), 6(i), 8(g), 9(d), 9(f), 10(e), 10(g)
Use of data to support learning	5(k), 6(j-p), 7(l), 8(n), 8(o), 9(g), 9(h), 9(k)	6(q-v), 7(q), 8(s), 9(l)	2(d), 5(c), 5(f), 6(a-i), 8(b), 8(d), 8(g), 9(c), 9(f), 10(a-c)

*Cross-disciplinary skills

InTASC Model Core Teaching Standards Update Committee

Mary Diez, Co-Chair
Dean, School of Education, Alverno College

Peter McWalters, Co-Chair
Consultant, Commissioner of Education, Rhode Island (retired)

Kathleen Paliokas, Director
InTASC, Council of Chief State School Officers

David Paradise, Senior Associate
InTASC, Council of Chief State School Officers

- Richard Allan, Vice President, Evaluation Systems group of Pearson
- Katherine Bassett, Director, Educator Relations Group, Educational Testing Service (Teacher of the Year – New Jersey)
- Victoria Chamberlain, Executive Director, Oregon Teacher Standards and Practices Commission
- Pamela Coleman, Director of Teacher Education and Licensure, Kansas State Department of Education
- Lynne Cook, Professor of Special Education, California State University, Dominguez Hills
- Manuel Cox, Lead Teacher, Engineering Academy for Student Excellence (EASE), American High School (NBCT)
- Nadene Davidson, Interim Head, Department of Teaching, University of Northern Iowa (NBCT)
- Sydnee Dickson, Director, Teaching and Learning, Utah State Office of Education
- Karen Huffman, Assistant Superintendent, Division of Educator Quality, West Virginia Department of Education
- Maria Hyler, Assistant Professor, University of Maryland, College Park (NBCT)
- Susan Johnsen, Professor in the Department of Educational Psychology and Director of the PhD Program, School of Education, Baylor University
- Carlene Kirkpatrick, Instructional Coach, DeKalb County School System (NBCT)
- Jean Miller, Consultant, Council of Chief State School Officers
- Antoinette Mitchell, Interim Dean, School of Education, Trinity Washington University
- Gwen Wallace Nagel, Director, Iowa Learning Online, Iowa Department of Education
- Richelle Patterson, Senior Policy Analyst, Teacher Quality Department, National Education Association
- Irving Richardson, Coordinator for Public Education and School Support NEA-NH (Teacher of the Year - Maine)
- Maria del Carmen Salazar, Assistant Professor, Curriculum and Instruction Morgridge College of Education, University of Denver
- Theodore Small, 5th grade teacher, Clark County School District, Nevada
- Afi Y. Wiggins, PhD Candidate, Research Statistics and Evaluation, Curry School of Education, University of Virginia

NBCT – National Board Certified Teacher

Made in United States
North Haven, CT
22 July 2022

21704601R00015